CHASING THE ALPHABET

THE STORY OF CHILDREN'S AUTHOR

JERRY PALLOTTA

By Pamela Ryan

About the Author Books

1994

This book is based on interviews, research, and location observations and was written with the cooperation and authorization of Jerry Pallotta, his family, and others mentioned in the text. All events described in the book are true. No part of this book has been fictionalized.

Published by
Shining Sea Press
P.O. Box 242
Boston, MA 02113

Library of Congress
Catalog Card Number 92-71704
ISBN 0-9634965-0-6

Printed in the United States of America
10 9 8 7 6 5 4 3 2 1

For MBA,
you're one in a zillion

Thank you to my editor, Mike Morley

CONTENTS

Chapter 1

"...it was like a dream."

In February of 1992, Jerry Pallotta drove to the California desert. Jerry loved the desert. He loved the cactuses, the Joshua trees, and the rocky mountains surrounding the Coachella Valley. This part of the country was so different from his home in Massachusetts, he imagined he could be on another planet. He was especially glad to have the chance to visit the southwest because he was working on *The Desert*

Alphabet Book, his fourteenth book.

Jerry was on his way to Cathedral City, California, near Palm Springs. He had been in California for ten days visiting schools and talking about his alphabet books to teachers, parents and hundreds of children. This would be his last stop before heading home.

He had been invited to be the grand marshall in the Sunny Sands Elementary School Reading Parade. He would be the honored guest for the day. He was very flattered that they chose him to be grand marshall. He thought this would be a nice school to visit and the reading parade sounded like fun. But Jerry Pallotta was in for a surprise. He had no idea how much fun was waiting for him.

The students in each grade dressed as characters from one of Jerry's books. One grade was underwater creatures. Another was reptiles. Another was bugs. And another was dinosaurs. Can you imagine being the teacher of a class of third graders and trying to get thirty reptile costumes together?

When Jerry pulled into the parking lot

he saw children dressed as scorpions. He saw three octopuses walking together. He saw a mother tacking antennae onto a giant child-bug. Another child was dragging a paper lizard tail behind him. A group of giggling jellyfish walked by. Parents were hovering around the halls with video cameras, waiting for the parade to start.

Buses pulled up to the curbs and children from other schools filed out to watch the parade. The local television and newspaper photographers prepared their cameras while the Sheriff's Department blocked off the one mile parade route.

Jerry headed straight for the playground. Giggling, laughing children flocked around him, asking for his autograph.

"Hey, what's your name? Is it spider-head? NO? Is it goosefish?" kidded Jerry.

During the parade Jerry rode in a decorated golf cart. Neighbors, children, and parents watched hundreds of yucky, icky, wiggly, alphabet book creatures parade by.

After the parade, the 850 children of Sunny Sands Elementary School held an assembly for Jerry Pallotta. They sang to him. They put on a play for him. They gave him presents. Jerry thanked them with some of his unusual assembly tricks. He put lobster claws on the principal's nose and turned a child upside-down like an Upside-down Jellyfish. The teachers laughed. The children really laughed.

Later, when asked about this day, Jerry said, "Remember when you were little and you looked forward to something for a long time? You would be so excited. And then the day came and it was better than you imagined - so much better that it was like a dream. That's how I felt that day."

Jerry Pallotta was 38 years old when he was the grand marshall of The Reading Parade. He started writing when he was 32 years old. This is the story of how, in six years, he carved a place for himself in the hearts and minds of children and teachers across the United States with his antics, his infectious child-like humor, and his unique alphabet books.

Chapter 2

"We slept in our bathing suits."

Jerry was born on March 26, 1953 to Joe and Mary Pallotta. His real name is Gerard Larry Pallotta but everyone has always called him Jerry. He is the second oldest of seven children. He has four brothers, Joe, David, Andrew and Danny. He also has two sisters, Cindy and Mickey. That may seem like a lot, but Jerry has always thought it was fun being a part of a big family.

Although Jerry lived in Medford,

Massachusetts, he claims he did his real growing up on Peggotty Beach. Peggotty Beach is in Scituate, Massachusetts, twenty-five miles south of Boston. Peggotty is a sandy shore bordered by two cliffs called Second Cliff and Third Cliff. The north end of the shore is crowded with boulders and the south end flattens out into a pebble beach. Every June, on the day that school got out, Jerry's mother packed a suitcase full of bathing suits and the family moved to the beach house until September.

"I can remember that we lived in our bathing suits. We slept in our bathing suits," said Jerry. His mother admits that the easiest way to get seven children ready for their next day on the beach was to put them in clean bathing suits after their baths each night.

Their house was big and the back yard was sand all the way to the ocean. There was always an old boat in the yard to play in and plenty of playmates because, besides his brothers and sisters, Jerry had seventy-eight cousins! Jerry's grandmother and several aunts and uncles had houses next to his and often there would be thirty or forty relatives at the beach at one time.

There was plenty of time for exploring the Scituate coastline. Jerry's favorite activity was "hanging on the rocks." This meant spending the day crawling around the boulder side of the beach searching for little green crabs, big rock crabs, starfish, mussels, little eels, periwinkles and sea urchins.

Some of Jerry's fondest memories were of clamming at Rivermoor, beyond the bend of Third Cliff. When Jerry's grandmother found odd shoes left on the beach, she saved them for clamming. She threw them into a bushel basket in her cellar. None of them matched but it didn't matter. She knew that when the tide was low the grandchildren would come looking for old sneakers to clam in, saving their good shoes from the mucky sand.

"We must have been a sight walking around the beach," said Jerry. "There might be thirty of us wearing shoes from my grandmother's basket - some with two left shoes and others with one red and one blue.

I remember wearing shoes that were way too big or much too small, but it was fun. We learned to recognize the clam holes in the damp sand. We just scooped down into the sand with our hands and found the soft-shelled clams called steamers."

Jerry and his brothers often went deep-sea fishing with their father. Mary Pallotta packed them a lunch and they spent the day on the ocean. They often caught little sharks, called dogfish. Jerry was afraid of them. He thought they could bite the anchor line and pull the boat all the way to England. He wouldn't look over the edge of the boat because he thought a dogfish might jump out of the water and bite his head off. He even had nightmares about them. When he grew older, he was surprised to learn that dogfish are shy and afraid of people!

On rare occasions they caught a wolffish. The jaws of a wolffish are strong enough to crack open clams and mussels. Jerry remembers his father warning him about the danger of a wolffish's bite. Once, when Jerry caught a wolffish, his father put a broom handle in its mouth and the wolffish bit it in two!

Growing up on Peggotty Beach had a tremendous impact on Jerry Pallotta's life. He chased minnows in the marshy creek behind his house. He examined jellyfish and hid little green crabs in his pockets. He fished and clammed. He chased sea gulls and sandpipers and watched terns and cormorants dive for their dinner. His summers were full of long days on the beach and, although he didn't know it at the time, he was already researching his first book!

Chapter
3

"Incredible things came out of the ocean!"

The ocean brought many interesting and peculiar things to the Scituate coastline. Something unusual always washed ashore on Peggotty Beach. Once, Jerry found a dead goosefish on shore. Goosefish have mouths as wide as their bodies. Jerry was curious about the goosefish so his Uncle Sonny cut open the stomach and inside was an entire bird, a large sea gull, dead of course.

Another time, Jerry and his brothers

found a bottle floating near the rocks. There was a message inside! A government agency had set it afloat months earlier as an experiment to study the ocean currents. Jerry and his brothers got a reward for writing back and telling the agency where they found the bottle.

One day Jerry walked from Peggotty Beach to the Scituate town pier. Four men in a little boat had been out fishing and caught a tuna - a three thousand pound tuna! They could not lift it into their small boat so they tied a rope around its tail and dragged it to the pier. There was a lot of discussion about how to get the tuna out of the water. Finally, someone called a tow truck. Jerry watched the fishermen tie the tow truck hook to the tuna's tail and hoist it out of the water. The fisherman sold the tuna to a fish cannery for eight thousand dollars!

"Incredible things came out of the ocean. We were always hearing about something. Then we would have to go see it to believe it," said Jerry.

This was especially true after an enormous cargo ship was blown so far off course during a hurricane that it ran aground at Scituate Harbor next to the Scituate lighthouse. Jerry remembers his parents taking him into Scituate to see the ship that seemed bigger than the harbor itself.

Sometimes Jerry spent the day with local fishermen on commercial fishing boats called draggers. Once, when a load of fish was being dropped on deck, a human skull tumbled from the pile of fish and landed at Jerry's feet. When the boat got back to shore, the captain called the police and the authorities measured the skull to try and determine the identity.

He remembers a particular catch of fish that would not stop jumping around the deck. When he took a closer look, he noticed a huge gray ray among the fish. Jerry tried to get close to it but the captain yelled, "Get away!" It was a numbfish, sometimes called an electric ray or Atlantic torpedo fish. The fish were jumping because they were electrocuted when their bodies touched the ray. "I remember the captain had to put

19

on rubber gloves and boots to get close to the ray," said Jerry. "He stopped the boat and shoved the ray off the deck with a broom. He was very careful. One touch and the ray could numb his arm or leg."

Sea creatures weren't the only things to appear in the fishermen's catch. Unfortunately, some people have used the ocean as a garbage can. Jerry saw soda cans, bottles and all sorts of trash come out of the ocean.

Jerry said, "It was sad. I learned to appreciate how important it is to keep our oceans clean. People don't realize that what goes overboard can be moved by the strong ocean currents and can make it back to the areas where we swim. The ocean can move almost anything!"

One incident is especially clear in Jerry's memory. One day, when he and his brothers and cousins were playing on the rocks, they noticed something dark bobbing adrift on the water. It was too far away to identify so they rowed out for a closer look.

News announcers had reported that a

huge leatherback turtle was lost along the coast of Massachusetts. The Pallottas were excited because they thought they had found the lost turtle. As they got closer they were shocked to see that, what they thought was a leatherback turtle, was a bloated dead body floating on the water. They rowed back to Peggotty Beach and told Jerry's parents. There was no phone in the beach house so Mr. Pallotta called the Coast Guard from a neighbor's house. They found out later that the body was that of an inexperienced fisherman who had drowned a few weeks earlier.

Jerry said, "We learned to respect the power of the ocean at a very young age. We played in groups and when we went out in our boats, we were prepared. We had anchors and life preservers. We were good swimmers but we didn't swim alone."

For children spending their summers near the water, these were wise and practical rules to live by. Although he was always intrigued and curious about the discoveries on Peggotty Beach, Jerry admits he was both comfortable and cautious around the ocean.

Chapter 4

"What a job!"

If you were to ask Jerry Pallotta, "What's the best job you ever had before you began writing books?" he would say, "Mossing." Mossing is harvesting seaweed.

Jerry harvested the seaweed by raking it off the rocks that were under the water. Mossing rakes are sixteen feet long and have thirty-two brass teeth. Jerry could only moss during the two hours before low tide and the two hours after. Otherwise, the water level was too high to snag the seaweed with the mossing rakes. He harvested a seaweed called Irish Sea Moss. It looks like brown broccoli with very skinny stems.

When Jerry was fourteen, his father bought him a dory. A dory is a wooden work boat that looks like a canoe with high sides. He and his brothers had Lucien dories made by a local man named Lucien Rousseau. Their dories had square backs instead of curved, pointed ends. Jerry and his brothers and cousins often rowed along the Scituate coastline to moss together at spots called Two Sisters, Doherty's Cove, Long Ledge, Harvey's Cove, Martha and Arthur, and Lighthouse Point. Jerry's favorite mossing spots were Smith Rocks and Third Cliff.

After four hours of mossing, Jerry's dory was full of seaweed. Then he rowed back to the harbor to have the seaweed weighed. He received a slip of paper that listed how much seaweed he harvested for that day and every two weeks he was paid. In those days, he got 2 or 3 cents for each pound of seaweed.

The seaweed was then sold to a company that made it into carrageen. Carrageen is a stabilizer that keeps ingredients mixed together. It is sometimes used in products such as ice cream, chocolate milk, whipped cream, hand lotion, and toothpaste.

If a boy had an outboard motor on his boat, he could tow other boats out to the mossing spots and then tow them back in at the end of the day. But sometimes the boats were so loaded with seaweed that, even with a tow, it could take two hours to get back to the dock.

If a dory was too full of seaweed it might sink. Jerry's dory did sink once. Jerry had turned into Harvey's Cove, out of sight of the other mossers. He was raking moss off of sheer rock cliffs, in deep water, when a wave shoved his dory into a submerged rock ledge. The wooden floorboard cracked and water began flooding the dory. The boat was already riding low because Jerry was carrying about 1500 pounds of seaweed. Water began rushing over the sides of his dory and Jerry realized he was sinking. If the boat flipped over, he knew he could get caught in the net and be trapped underwater. He had to get out of the boat!

"There was a lot of competition among the mossers," said Jerry. "I knew I had a good load of moss. I didn't want to have a bad day but I didn't want to drown either."

He jumped overboard and held onto the side of the listing dory, steadying it straight in the water. Waves began breaking over the dory and washing the seaweed into the surf. He was losing pounds of seaweed with each wave but he was able to keep the boat level. By pushing off the rock ledges with his legs, Jerry was able to edge his dory along the cliffs toward the small beach at the end of the cove.

Fortunately, another mosser rounded the corner of the inlet and saw Jerry. He helped Jerry to the beach and Jerry bailed the water out of his dory. He only had about 300 pounds of seaweed left in the hull of the dory. His friend towed him back to Scituate. It had been a disappointing day. He would have made $45.00 for his haul but ended up with only $9.00.

Jerry was a dedicated mosser. If the water was cloudy from choppy seas, he mossed off the shoreline at the big rocks called ledges. He lived for the days when the ocean was "flat calm," the water was clear, and there was an abundant crop. Those were the days he could harvest the most seaweed. It was unusual for a mosser to rake over a ton (2000 pounds) of seaweed in one day but Jerry did it four times, once pulling in 2,420 pounds. He still holds a record for raking over 1000 pounds of seaweed ten days in a row and for raking 50,000 pounds three summers in a row.

He still remembers his greatest mossing day ever. It was dark when he left at four in the morning. He and his brothers and cousins - eight of them - each in their own dory, headed out to moss. One boy was towing the seven other boats.

Jerry said, "It looked like a line of ducks heading into the dawn. We saw the sun come up. The ocean was flat calm, like a mirror. We raked until around ten in the morning then we headed back in to unload. It was a double low tide that day. About three in the afternoon we headed out again and raked until sunset. The sky was streaked with unbelievable colors and the ocean was still flat calm. Then we saw the moon come up over the bay. We all had loaded dories. They were so full that it took until after dark to get back to the dock. I still remember the whole day and my brothers and I still talk about it. I remember thinking, 'What a job!'"

Jerry sometimes spent up to eight hours a day on the ocean in his dory. Sometimes he and his brothers slept in their docked dories. Jerry loved being outside, on the water, getting the sun's reflections from the sea. He liked being in his bathing suit all day. He liked knowing all the guys who mossed and kidding around with them. And, he especially liked having his own dory and being responsible for himself.

Jerry said, "My father used to tell me that mossing was like life – that the guys that were good at mossing would be good at life.

I think he was right. There were a lot of circumstances that could affect your success
each day – the weather, the tides, which spot
you chose, who you mossed with, even your
own moods. I was taught to go out and do
my best no matter what the conditions were."

Jerry mossed every summer during high
school. Then he went to Georgetown
University in Washington D.C. During his
college years, his parents moved to the beach
house permanently and Jerry went home to
Peggotty each summer to moss. Before he
graduated from college he had saved
enough money from mossing to buy his first
house.

Date 6/22/ 19 74

M G. Pallotta

No.

Reg. No.	Clerk	ACCOUNT FORWARDED			
1					
2					
3					
4					
5	2040				
6					
7					
8					
9	Rousseau				
10					
11					
12					
13					
14					
15	43				

30

Chapter 5

"A is not always for Apple"

When Jerry went to college at Georgetown University he met his future wife, Linda Owens. Linda and Jerry got married after they graduated from college and almost two years later Sheila Pallotta was born. Then came Neil, Eric and Jill.

Linda encouraged Jerry to read to the children. She was an English major in college and she wanted her children to love books. Jerry noticed that the alphabet books were all similar. Different authors wrote them and different publishers printed them and they were different sizes and shapes, but they seemed all the same. *A* was always for *Apple,* *U* was always for *Umbrella,* and *Z* was always for *Zebra.*

Jerry even had an argument with Sheila when he tried to substitute different words while he read to her from one of the alphabet books. Sheila stubbornly insisted, "Daddy, A is ALWAYS for Apple!"

Jerry stubbornly insisted, "*A* is NOT ALWAYS for Apple!" Jerry was frustrated. He thought there had to be another way to write about the alphabet. He decided he could write an alphabet book that was different.

Jerry wanted to do an alphabet book on Peggotty Bay from his own experiences. Traditional alphabet books have no information about each word. Jerry wanted to include text along with each letter, so children could learn about Peggotty Bay. He began making notes on a yellow note pad. He had the alphabet book half written when he lost the yellow pad.

"I couldn't find it anywhere," said Jerry. "I was selling insurance at the time and was very busy so I didn't think too much about it. A few months later I picked up a piece of paper and started making notes again, this time I was determined to finish and print a book."

Jerry found he could do most of the alphabet letters on Peggotty Bay by writing about many of the things he was familiar with as a child. He used goosefish, lobster, periwinkle, urchin, eel, dogfish and others. Then he decided to write about the North Atlantic Ocean so that he could include other interesting creatures, like viperfish, killer whales, and octopuses.

After he completed the book, he began looking for an illustrator, someone to draw the pictures for each page. Jerry was lucky in several ways. First, his cousin Frank Mazzola, Jr., had just graduated from art school. Jerry told him about his idea to make a book and asked Frank to draw the pictures. Second, Jerry's brother, Andrew, was in the color printing business and told Jerry that he could print the book when it was ready.

It never occurred to Jerry to look for a publisher. A publisher is a company that hires the illustrator, prints the book, advertises the book, sells the book to the stores, and pays the money to have all of these things done.

Jerry did not know one thing about publishing at that time. He thought that if you wanted to write a book you did it all yourself. "I can only assume that this attitude came from the fact that everyone in my family worked for themselves and that my father always told me I could accomplish anything." said Jerry.

Frank began working on the illustrations. His brother, Andrew, was waiting to print the pages when they were ready. Jerry was on his way to publishing his first book, but he still had a lot of questions. How would he sell the books to stores? How many should he print? How many pages should the book be? Would anyone buy it? Despite his concerns Jerry never once considered turning back. And what Jerry didn't know was that he would soon be sitting at dinner with someone who had the answers to his questions.

Chapter
6

"I'll take five thousand..."

About the time that Jerry was wrestling with the idea of printing *The Ocean Alphabet Book*, he was invited to a fundraising dinner for the high school he attended, Boston College High School. Jerry knew many people there from the class he graduated with, but there were also many people there older and younger than he. When it came time to sit down for dinner, there were no places left at the table with his friends so Jerry sat at a table with a group of people he didn't know.

Jerry sat right next to a gentleman named Henry Quinlan. Henry introduced himself and said, "I'm a publisher."

Jerry said, "I'm working on a children's book."

Jerry couldn't believe his good fortune. During the rest of the evening, Henry Quinlan gave Jerry a lot of advice about publishing books. Later in the week, he invited Jerry to his office to discuss publishing further. Henry was very interested in helping Jerry but advised him to do some marketing research first. In this case, marketing research meant finding out if anyone would buy the book after it was printed.

Henry encouraged him to make a color flyer, an advertisement, that showed what the book would look like. Jerry took his advice. He printed a flyer with his brother's help that showed the cover of the book and the octopus page. Henry Quinlan allowed Jerry to put "Quinlan Press" on the flyer. With Henry's endorsement and the color flyer, Jerry was ready to find out if anyone would buy his book.

Jerry thought the New England Aquarium would be a good place to start. He went to the gift shop but the clerk would not let him talk to the manager. The clerk said the manager would not speak to any salesman. Jerry walked back to the parking lot feeling like he didn't get a chance. As he pulled out of the parking lot, he noticed that the gift shop closed at four o'clock. He decided to come back right before closing to try one more time, and he hoped the clerk would no longer be there.

At five minutes before four o'clock, Jerry slipped into the New England Aquarium as everyone was leaving. He got to the gift shop just as they were pulling down the giant steel grates that closed the shop. He began rattling the grates to get someone's attention. Ellen Davis, the gift shop manager pretended to be closing out the register and ignored Jerry. She thought he was another tourist trying to buy a last minute souvenir. Jerry reached through the grates and waved the flyer at her and finally she walked over to talk to him. Jerry gave her the flyer and she glanced at it and said she wasn't interested. Again, Jerry was asked to leave. This time he left feeling very dejected. He was almost to the aquarium's front doors when he felt a tug on his shoulder. Ellen Davis had caught up with him.

She said, "Wait! I looked at your flyer and I thought about it. I'll take five thousand of these books."

Ellen Davis had reconsidered in the short time it took Jerry to walk to the front doors. There were no children's books in the gift shop at that time and Ellen realized how many children visited the aquarium each year with their parents. Jerry's timing was perfect but it was not just luck that got him his first order. It was also his perseverance.

He drove straight to Henry Quinlan's office and announced, "Marketing research is over!"

Jerry was on his way. He printed the first 10,000 copies of *The Ocean Alphabet Book* and began selling not only to the New England

Aquarium but to other aquariums and national parks around the country. Again, Henry Quinlan gave Jerry some valuable advice. He encouraged him to "look beyond the ocean."

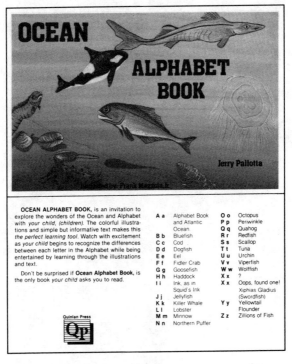

The flyer, featuring *The Ocean Alphabet Book*, that Jerry took to the New England Aquarium.

Chapter 7

"...two gifts from God."

A neighborhood bully once told Jerry that earwigs would crawl inside his ear and bite his brain. It made sense to Jerry. After all, earwig had the word "ear" in it. He also believed that dragonflies were "sewing needle bugs" and could stitch his mouth shut. He always worried about how he would breath if that happened. Jerry had vivid and sometimes scary memories about bugs from his childhood. At the same time, he was always fascinated by them.

After *The Ocean Alphabet Book,* Jerry thought about writing an alphabet book on bugs. He did some research to find out if such a book existed. He looked in libraries and bookstores and museum gift shops. He never found one. That was all the inspiration he needed to start writing his next book.

Again, Jerry began looking for an illustrator. Someone gave him Ralph Masiello's business card. Jerry was driving home one day, intrigued with the small illustration on the card. He intended to call Ralph as soon as he got home but the card flew out the window and disappeared in the wind. Jerry took a chance that Ralph would be listed with information and luckily got in touch with him. They met a few days later at a pancake restaurant and Jerry arranged for Ralph to paint a sample picture of a bumblebee and a cricket. Jerry loved them.

"I couldn't believe that I found Ralph, especially after losing his business card. His illustrations were exactly what I was looking for. I realized when I saw the bee and the cricket that he was a terrific painter. What really surprised me was how much fun he was to work with."

One evening, during the time that Ralph was illustrating the bug book, Jerry and his son Neil were playing a lotto matching game. Neil matched two elephant stag beetles but refused to pick up his match because, as Neil said, "they're icky." It occurred to Jerry that this was a typical child-like feeling and response. He decided to call his book, *The "Icky" Bug Alphabet Book* and since Neil thought of it, Jerry gave him credit for the title. The title page in the book reads, "*The Icky Bug Alphabet Book* by Jerry Pallotta, Title by Neil Pallotta." That is also why the elephant stag beetle appears on the title page of *The Icky Bug Alphabet Book*.

Neil's title did not just stick on the *Icky Bug Alphabet Book*, though. Everywhere Jerry Pallotta went, he referred to his illustrator as The Icky Bug Man. The name stuck. Although Ralph Masiello is a fine artist as well as an illustrator, and sells exquisite paintings in galleries around the United States, he is known by children and teachers as The Icky Bug Man.

During the production of *The Icky Bug Alphabet Book* Jerry visited Drumlin Farm at the Audubon Society Headquarters in Lincoln, Massachusetts. The Audubon Society is an organization that focuses on the conservation of the natural world, including birds. Drumlin Farm is a wonderful place to bring young children. It has animals and a beautiful gift shop with extraordinary nature books. Jerry took his children there one afternoon and noticed there were no children's alphabet books on birds so, true to form, he began *The Bird Alphabet Book*. Since Ralph was busy on the bug book, Jerry needed another illustrator.

Henry Quinlan recommended Edgar Stewart, so Jerry went to meet him and to see his work. Jerry was impressed with the samples he saw hanging in Edgar's office, especially the portraits. Edgar did a sample of the Atlantic Puffins and Jerry hired him to do the bird book, although the original Atlantic Puffin painting never made it to the final copy. What Jerry didn't know at the time was that Edgar loved birds and knew a lot about their habitats. He even drew birds when he was a young boy growing up in rural Vermont. After Edgar illustrated the bird book, the Audubon Society reviewed his drawings and checked the bird's colors, their bodies, and their habitats for accuracy. Edgar's drawings were flawless.

Jerry had fun working on books with Edgar and Ralph. They are all talented and creative in different ways. They brainstorm ideas and the finished products are beautifully illustrated, factual books for children and teachers.

Jerry said, "It's hard to express in words how lucky I was to find Edgar and Ralph. They became my team. And to think of the circumstances that brought me to them. I lost Ralph's card and I possibly might not have tried to reach him again. And imagine finding an illustrator for a bird book who loved birds! It's a miracle, really. They were my two gifts from God."

Chapter
8

"...a long way from Peggotty Beach Books."

It was 1987 and Jerry was his own publisher. He imprinted "Peggotty Beach Books" on his books and his logo was a silhouette of a boy mossing in a dory.

PEGGOTTY BEACH BOOKS

Jerry was doing all the work. He wrote the books, designed them, edited them, hired his own illustrators, printed the books, advertised the books, took all the orders and shipped the books - all out of an office in the basement of his house! The books were selling very well but he was putting the profits, the extra money he made on the books, into reprinting his titles and into paying illustrators for new books. With a young family to support, he could not afford to promote his books nationwide or to leave his insurance job.

"At that time I would have loved to have quit insurance and just done books. Anybody would. My mind was going a mile a minute with ideas."

In fact, Henry Quinlan said, "Jerry had so many ideas it was like watching steam come out of his head."

At this point Jerry realized that with a growing line of books he could not do everything: write the books, promote the books, package them and ship them out of his basement, come up with new ideas, and sell insurance too. He published *The Ocean Alphabet Book, The Icky Bug Alphabet Book, The Bird Alphabet Book, The Flower Alphabet Book,* and was working on *The Yucky Reptile Alphabet Book* when Charlesbridge Publishing came into his life.

Jerry was introduced to Brent Farmer by a friend. Brent was the president of Charlesbridge Publishing. Jerry made an appointment to meet with him. He realized that this could be an opportunity of a lifetime. He went to the meeting prepared. He brought his published books, records of his sales, and his ideas and plans for other alphabet books. At that time Charlesbridge was only selling books to schools and they had no color picture books to sell to stores and bookshops. Jerry had color picture books that were selling in stores and bookshops but he was not selling any books in the schools. This was a perfect opportunity for Jerry and Charlesbridge to grow. Charlesbridge asked to publish Jerry's books and Jerry signed with them in September of 1988. The first book of Jerry's that Charlesbridge published was *The Yucky Reptile Alphabet Book.*

Being with a publisher had its advantages and one of those advantages was Mary Ann Sabia, the Marketing Director at Charlesbridge. Mary Ann's job was to think of ways to promote the books that made people want to buy them. She designed flyers, advertisements, catalog pages, buttons, and she thought of ways to get stores interested in buying the books. She also hired people to sell Jerry's books to bookstores all around the country. For the first time, Jerry's books were printed in hardcover instead of just paperback.

"The day I signed with Charlesbridge I was relieved. Now I had a publisher with nationwide distribution. Someone who would help me promote my books with a catalog and sales people that went all over the country. Now someone else was interested in my future books. I felt like I had come a long way from Peggotty Beach Books."

Chapter
9

"...research was serious stuff..."

Now that Jerry had a publisher, he could devote more time to research and working with the illustrators. Jerry would decide on an idea for a book, choose an illustrator, and then start considering the words for each alphabet letter.

Ralph Masiello never hesitated to accept the chance to illustrate any of Jerry's books, except the frog book. Ralph had a terrible hatred of frogs. When Ralph was a little boy, his brother and another boy put him in a rabbit cage with a bunch of bullfrogs and latched the door. Then they pushed it down a hill. Rabbit droppings, straw, frightened bullfrogs and poor Ralph were all tumbled together.

Ralph said, "By the time the cage stopped rolling, frogs were hopping all over me. They eventually let me out of the cage but I NEVER liked frogs after that."

Jerry was very convincing and begged Ralph to do the book and promised him he would not have to work from live specimens. People frequently ask Ralph if illustrating the frog book helped him get over his fear of frogs. He says emphatically, "NO!"

One day, while researching *The Frog Alphabet Book,* Jerry walked into the Herpetology Department at Harvard University, in Cambridge, Massachusetts, where they study reptiles and amphibians. He was after one thing - feet. He and Ralph had been searching through encyclopedias, National Geographic magazines, books on amphibians, and The Guiness Book of World

Records to see a picture of the feet of the goliath frog for the G page in *The Frog Alphabet Book*. The goliath frog is the biggest frog in the world. They could not locate a picture of a goliath frog that showed the feet, and Jerry and Ralph were determined to have factually accurate illustrations as well as text. Jerry decided to ask the experts.

José Rosado, Van Wallach and Franklin Ross, at Harvard, got out their frog books. They looked in frog books from Belgium that told about the reptiles and amphibians of the Cameroons, West Africa, where the goliath frog comes from. But the experts from Harvard couldn't find a picture of the feet of the goliath frog either.

Then Franklin Ross had an idea. He told Jerry, "Follow me," and he walked over to a specimen jar the size of a trash barrel. He put his arm in the jar, which was full of alcohol, and pulled out a dead, preserved goliath frog. Then he walked out of the room. There was nothing Jerry could do but follow him. They walked down corridors and hallways and out of the building. Jerry found himself walking with Franklin Ross, a herpetology expert, across Harvard's campus with a goliath frog dangling between them.

Franklin finally arrived at his destination, a copy machine. He spread out one foot of the goliath frog and placed it on the glass. Being careful to avoid parts of the copier that might be damaged by the alcohol-soaked frog leg, he pushed the START button. Out came a beautiful copy of the goliath frog's foot. Then he did the other foot. Franklin looked at Jerry and said, "There are your feet."

Franklin Ross helped Jerry with another letter in *The Frog Alphabet Book*, the U. Jerry walked into Franklin's office one day and said, "Franklin, I'm missing a U."

Franklin said, "Here's your U, right here! See this tray of frogs? These are unnamed frogs."

Franklin explained to Jerry that new species of frogs are frequently discovered as rain forests are cut down. Unusual frogs appear that no one has ever seen because they have been hidden for generations in plants growing on branches high up in the forest canopy, the top of the rainforest. These frogs are sent to scientists to be categorized. Jerry and Franklin discussed how unfortunate it was to make a discovery through the destruction of a valuable rain forest. The forests are being cut down so fast that some plant and animal species are going extinct before people have time to study them! Jerry eventually found a frog with a name that started with the letter U, but he used "U is for Undiscovered Frog," as a favor to Franklin Ross.

The most difficult letter in *The Frog Alphabet Book* was the Q. The Harvard experts and Jerry spent weeks looking under Latin names, species names, and common names for frogs and amphibians searching for one that started with the letter Q. There simply wasn't one. Jerry thought he was going to have to write, "We searched and searched but couldn't find a frog that starts with the letter Q."

Finally, Franklin Ross found the frog *Hyla quitoe* in a book. Franklin explained that Hyla means "tree frog" and *Hyla quitoe* means "the tree frog from Quito", Ecuador. Although this scientific name was only used for this frog from 1913 to 1972, Franklin and Jerry agreed that the English version, Quito Tree Frog, was the answer to Jerry's Q problem.

"These guys were fabulous to me," said Jerry. "I've been pleasantly surprised at the sincerity and help I have encountered from the people at museums and universities. I have observed live animals, I have been loaned books and shown specimens. I wanted to get the facts straight and to portray the exciting side of nature and the experts I have worked with never took it lightly. We all thought research was serious stuff - even for an alphabet book!"

Jerry, next to a Dimetrodon at the
Museum of Comparative Zoology.

Goliath Frog specimens.

Jerry said, "I got an eerie feeling standing next to the fossilized remains of a dinosaur that lived millions of years ago."

Chapter 10

"You never know what you will find."

Lobster traps, sometimes called pots, are wooden crates baited with smelly fish. When Jerry was in high school, he also used his dory to go lobstering. He dropped his traps underwater at the beginning of each summer. Buoys marked the locations of his traps and he could tell his buoys by the colors. His buoy colors were green, white, and red. He checked his traps every day hoping for a lobster catch, but he didn't just catch lobsters.

61

Once, he began pulling the rope connected to one of his lobster traps. It weighed much more than usual. His arms ached from pulling the trap through the water. He couldn't imagine what he had caught that could weigh so much. He struggled to hoist the trap onto his dory. It was stuffed with rock crabs. As he tossed them back into the ocean, he counted two hundred and fifty-eight crabs that had crawled into one lobster trap!

Another time he pulled his trap aboard and found hundreds of tiny hermit crabs inside. They began inching out of the trap and were soon crawling around the floorboards of the dory. "They were the size of marbles and each had its own unique shell. They were everywhere," said Jerry. "I had to catch them, one by one, and put them back into the ocean. It was fun!"

As strange as it seems, he once caught a shark in a lobster trap, too. Jerry thinks that lobstering is like hunting for sunken treasure because you are often in for a surprise when the trap gets to the surface.

"I had the idea for writing *Going Lobstering* right after I finished *The Ocean Alphabet Book* but I got sidetracked on my other books," said Jerry. "It ended up being my seventh book, I wanted to show a story of ten lobster traps and ten different things that could be found inside because that's how lobstering is. You never know what you will find."

The *Going Lobstering* book is a sentimental favorite of Jerry's. It tells about lobstering, which was a part of his life, and Big Joe in *Going Lobstering* is Jerry's father, Joe Pallotta. Mr. Pallotta is not a lobsterman in real life. He is a businessman who owns a nursing home. He has spent plenty of time out on the water though, pulling in lobster traps during the years he vacationed on Peggotty Bay. Another reason Jerry loves this book is that Sheila and Neil, his oldest children, are the children that appear in the book and the father in the book is Jerry's good friend, Frank Mastrocola. The first and second pages of the book show Peggotty Beach, the place Jerry remembers as his childhood home.

Rob Bolster illustrated the *Going Lobstering* book. He was an advertising illustrator in Boston when Jerry' wife and Rob's wife got them together. It took Rob over three years to complete the book because he worked on it between his advertising jobs. It was worth waiting for. Rob's final illustrations were painstakingly beautiful. They are realistic renditions of Peggotty Beach, Big Joe, Neil and Sheila, and lobstering.

"I wanted children to feel like they were really there," said Rob. "I wanted them to know what a lobster looked like and to feel like they were part of the story."

Rob likes to illustrate from models and he needed a big lobster to pose for the gigantic lobster that is caught in the book. Jerry went to James Hook and Company, a lobster warehouse in downtown Boston, and asked the manager, Buddy Lynch, if he could borrow a lobster for an hour. Buddy thought this was a strange request. Jerry explained that they didn't want to eat the lobster or hurt it. They just wanted to take pictures of it. Buddy agreed and searched through several large tanks before he brought out one of the biggest lobsters Jerry had ever seen. It weighed over twenty pounds. Its claws were bigger than Jerry's feet! They carried it to a photo studio and Mr. Pallotta posed with the huge lobster while Rob took pictures. Rob used those pictures to get ideas for his illustrations.

Another time Rob needed a dogfish shark to look at. Rob's brother was a commercial fisherman and was out on the ocean when he got a ship-to-shore radio call from Rob and Jerry asking if he had any dogfish in his catch. Luckily, he did. He met them back at shore so that Rob could take reference pictures for the book.

When *Going Lobstering* was published, the local bookstore in Scituate had a reception and book signing for Jerry and Rob. Hundreds of local residents showed up to buy books. Joe Pallotta became somewhat of a celebrity and many people still think he is a lobsterman. Some of Rob Bolster's original art work from *Going Lobstering* hangs in Mary and Joe Pallotta's living room in their house on Peggotty Beach in Scituate.

Jerry was right when he said, "You never know what you will find in a lobster trap." In his case, he found an idea for a book.

Jerry and his daughter Jill on Nana Pallotta's porch with a huge lobster.

Jerry and Molly Schecter, principal of Sunny Sands Elementary
School, after the Reading Parade in 1992.

Jerry, age 6 months.

First grade.

Seventh grade.

Jerry's senior picture from Boston College High School.

The Italian freighter "Etrusco" ran aground at Scituate Harbor during a hurricane. The ship was later named the "Scituate."

Jerry's grandparents
on Peggotty Beach
with a striped bass that
was as tall as Jerry.

Jerry never realized how big a whale was until he stood on
Peggotty Beach next to a humpback whale that had died
and washed ashore.

Jerry, mossing in his dory.

Between mossing trips, Jerry's dory was moored in Peggotty Bay.

71

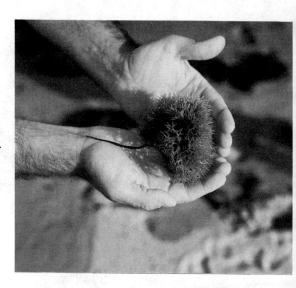

A sprig of Irish sea moss.

Frank Mazzola, Jr., illustrator of *The Ocean Alphabet Book*, also grew up on Peggotty Beach.

Edgar Stewart illustrated *The Bird Alphabet Book, The Furry Alphabet Book, The Underwater Alphabet Book,* and *The Victory Garden Alphabet Book.*

Leslie Evans, illustrator of *The Flower Alphabet Book,* with her dog, Morgan.

73

Instead of joining his family's construction business, Ralph
Masiello decided to become an artist. He loves to paint!
Now teachers and children know him as "The Icky Bug Man."
Ralph illustrated *The Icky Bug Alphabet Book, The Yucky Reptile
Alphabet Book, The Frog Alphabet Book, The Dinosaur Alphabet Book,
The Icky Bug Counting Book* and *The Extinct Alphabet Book.*

Jerry with Rob Bolster. Rob illustrated *Going Lobstering.*

The Victory Garden Alphabet Book "Team";
Edgar Stewart, illustrator, with Bob Thomson
and Jerry Pallotta.

When Jerry's sister, Cindy, got married, Jerry and his brothers showed up at the reception in full animal costumes. Jerry was the gorilla.

When Jerry's sister, Mickey, got married, Jerry and his brothers brought an elephant to the wedding reception.

76

G is for Goosefish. A Goosefish is ugly-looking. It has lots of teeth. Its mouth is as wide as its body. Goosefish are also called monkfish.

Gg

Jerry's sister, Mickey, and the illustration of the goosefish. Jerry thinks they look alike. Do you?

Uncle Tony did not have to petition to get Beckie into *this* book. She was invited.

Jerry, standing next to the giant alphabet book that covered the gymnasium wall in Hopkington, New Hampshire.

Jerry remembers the day a student, Jimmy wore a suit and tie to school because he heard a "famous author" was coming to visit.

Jerry visiting an elementary school.

This school in Natick, Massachusetts welcomed Jerry with a big message.

Jerry and his mother,
Mary Pallotta.

Jerry's pride and joy – The "Icky Bugs" Girls' Indoor Soccer Team.
Top: Coaches Pallotta, Vercollone and Kenney;
Middle: Tracy Prihoda, Kelly Fay, Becky Remsen, Sarah Daoust,
Siobhan Whyte;
Bottom: Sheila Pallotta, Andrea Vercollone, Lauren Pallotta,
Courtney Roche, Kathy Kenney.

80

Chapter
11

"...please, <u>anything</u> but X-ray..."

Sometimes Jerry has had to become a detective in order to find a word that starts with the letter X for an alphabet book. He has never given up easily. He has been known to read the entire X sections of several English and foreign language dictionaries searching for an X word. He has searched through old stacks of science and nature magazines. He has asked the help of experts. Sometimes, after a long search, he has given up completely before an X appears.

Jerry was at a school one day telling children about his books. He mentioned to a classroom of first graders that he was working on a dinosaur alphabet book. After his presentation, a boy came up to him and said, "You're in big trouble."

Jerry asked, "Why?"

The boy answered, "Because if you are doing a dinosaur alphabet book, you will never find an X dinosaur. I know all the dinosaurs in the world and there is no dinosaur that starts with the letter W or X."

Jerry was worried. While driving home, he was preoccupied with what the boy had said. He wondered if a first grader could be right. The minute he arrived home he got out his dinosaur books. They were up-to-date and accurate paleontology books that experts had recommended to him. He found a W dinosaur but he soon discovered that the boy was right. There was no X dinosaur in any of his books.

Jerry went back to Harvard University.

This time he was hunting for an X. He met Chuck Schaff, a dinosaur and prehistoric mammal expert. Chuck let Jerry look through dinosaur books from all over the world. Jerry began reading a dinosaur book from China. The boy was wrong. Jerry didn't find ONE dinosaur whose name started with the letter X. He found FIVE dinosaurs whose names started with the letter X! He decided on Xiaosaurus.

"I was so relieved," said Jerry, "All I could think of was that I had enough X's for four <u>more</u> dinosaur alphabet books!"

Sometimes Jerry finds an X word in an unlikely place. He has found X's in museums, in zoos, on posters in gift shops, on markers in nature preserves and on bulletin boards in classrooms.

Jerry found Xeranthemum (pronounced zeranthemum) for *The Flower Alphabet Book* after reading seed packets in a garden supply store.

"I'm sure the owner didn't know what to think of me. I was in the store in the middle of the day in my suit and tie, reading row upon row of seed packets. I was there for over an hour. The clerks kept asking if they could help me and I said I was just looking. When I found the xeranthemum packet, I was ecstatic! I'm sure the owner was disappointed, after spending all that time in his store, that I only purchased one 69 cent packet of seeds. But it was the only one I wanted. It was an X flower."

Jerry admits that some of the X's in his books have been more difficult to find than others. *The Furry Alphabet Book* is about land mammals and it was the hardest X, so far. When Jerry finally found xukazi, (pronounced zukazi), it was in a Zulu dictionary. A xukazi is a female lamb. At the same time, he discovered that the Xhosa (pronounced zoe-sa) people speak Zulu. Jerry decided to introduce the Xhosa people along with the xukazi on the X page of *The Furry Alphabet Book* so that, just for fun, he could have a DOUBLE X page.

Once, he thought he could not find an X. In his first book, *The Ocean Alphabet Book*, after months of searching, he wrote "We cannot think of any fish whose names begin with the letter X! Can you?" He told Frank Mazzola, Jr. to paint an empty water scene for that page. The book had already been sent to the printer when a librarian called from the New England Aquarium and told him that the scientific name for swordfish is *Xiphias gladius*. He left the page as it was originally written, but on the following page he wrote, "Oops, we found one! X is for *Xiphias gladius* (pronounced Ziphias). This is the scientific name for Swordfish."

"I was excited," said Jerry. "I was determined to have interesting words in my books. I wanted to get away from the traditional words that I had been reading from other alphabet books. Since my first book my attitude has always been, please, <u>anything</u> but x-ray on the X page!"

<u>Author's note:</u> While I was researching and writing this book, Jerry was desperately searching for an X for *The Extinct Alphabet Book*. He was ready to call an expert when I found the Xerces Blue, an extinct butterfly. I

was <u>thrilled</u> to call him with the news! He said, "Now you know how I feel when I find a great X!"

Chapter
12

"...from Mapleton to Chula Vista..."

Jerry has visited schools all around the country. He has been in the northeast corner of the United States in Mapleton, Maine. He has been in the southwest corner of the United States in Chula Vista, California, and he has been in many states in between. He has been in hundreds of classrooms and wherever he goes, he comes away with souvenirs, ideas for new alphabet books, inspiration from teachers and students, and once in a while he comes away with an extraordinary memory.

Many classes and schools have made alphabet books modeled after Jerry's series. In Hopkington, New Hampshire, an entire school made an ecology alphabet book. Maybe that doesn't seem remarkable but every page of their alphabet book was six feet high and six feet wide! The pages were mounted on the gymnasium wall. For instance, the letter <u>A</u> was for Aluminum Cans and that page had actual aluminum cans mounted on it. <u>P</u> was for Plastic and that page was covered in plastic bags. The <u>R</u> page was for Recycled Paper and samples of recycled paper were attached to it. Jerry was very impressed. Imagine twenty-six, six foot pages covering the walls of an entire gym!

"Visiting schools is the highlight of being a writer," says Jerry. "I've been from Mapleton to Chula Vista and I've found that when dealing with teachers and children you have to be prepared for a few surprises."

Once, when Jerry had started speaking to a class of children, the fire alarms went off.

It was an official fire drill run by the fire department. The school knew nothing about it. The children jumped up and began filing out of the room. Jerry was left standing in the front of the classroom holding up his books and a live lobster, until a teacher ran in and said, "Get out! They're timing us!"

Jerry ran out of the room and followed the children to the front of the school. He and the lobster lined up and were counted by the fire monitors along with everyone else, until the fire marshall announced, "All clear." The children thought it was funny that Jerry and the lobster were part of the fire drill. Jerry thought it was funny too, but admitted, "The lobster was a little nervous!"

One year, Jerry had a memorable birthday. He was scheduled to visit two schools and to talk to a teacher's group in the late afternoon. After he finished at the first school, the principal apologized and said, "Sorry Jerry, we have one more class for you to see." Jerry followed her through the school to the cafeteria. Three hundred children wearing party hats yelled, "Happy

Birthday Jerry!" They had a huge cake, a Birthday Alphabet Book, and about one hundred birthday cards. What a surprise!

At the next school, Jerry spoke to another group of children. After the assembly, he was escorted to a classroom and another surprise party! This time the teachers served cupcakes and made him a birthday crown. Later, when he spoke at the teacher's meeting, they gave him another cake! When he finally arrived home in the evening to celebrate his birthday with his family, the fourth cake was waiting for him. Yes, he managed to eat a piece of all four birthday cakes!

Once in a while Jerry comes across a school that he can't forget. One school is Mapleton Elementary in Mapleton, Maine. For two years, the teachers waited for Jerry Pallotta to speak at their school. One of the reading teachers had met Jerry at a conference and heard him speak. She went back to her school and began planning. Although the school had no funds for an author visit, the teachers began saving money by cooking breakfast and lunch for sportsmen in the area. It was an emotional moment for Jerry when he found out about their efforts. "They wanted to promote reading and writing by having an author at their school," he said. "They worked hard for two years to raise the money. I felt honored that they invited me."

Jerry also remembers Mapleton because he received an unusual gift there. On the first day of his visit, a young boy stood in line to meet Jerry. Some children were buying books. Jerry could tell the boy wanted a book but that he could not afford one. Jerry wanted to help him and told him that if he could find something from Maine and bring it to him the next day that he would trade him for a book. Jerry thought he might bring potatoes since Mapleton was surrounded by potato fields, or even fiddleheads, the uncurled ferns that people can eat.

The next day, the boy came to school carrying a cellophane bread bag. Inside was the gift for Jerry Pallotta. The children crowded around the boy to get a glimpse inside the bag. Since his father was a trapper, he had brought Jerry a skinned beaver's head. At first Jerry was shocked. He didn't like the idea that a beaver had been killed. He soon realized though, that this was something the boy was proud to trade him. Jerry remembers, "I traded him three books for the beaver's head. I signed the books and handed them to him and he handed me the bag. I'll never forget the look on his face. He walked away clutching the books with a crowd of kids following him. Suddenly, he was a celebrity. And there I was holding the bag with a beaver's head inside."

Jerry's problem was how to get it home. He finally decided to ship it home through overnight mail so he didn't have to take it on the plane. When he arrived home, the package was waiting for him. Now he had another problem. What should he do with a freshly skinned beaver's head? He thought the skull would be interesting to teachers and children. He took it to a friend's house and boiled it, and saved the delicate skull. For a few months he was able to take it around to schools and share it with other children. When the fragile teeth began breaking, he decided it was safer at home on his desk.

"Many children have given me gifts and teachers have done some amazing things to get me to their towns," said Jerry, "but I will never forget Mapleton, Maine...or Hopkington, New Hampshire...or Cathedral City, California...or..."

Chapter
13

"...a child trapped in a man's body."

Jerry was, and still is a practical joker – not in a mean way, but in a fun way. When Mickey, Jerry's sister, got married, he and his brothers hired a marching band to greet her and her new husband as they exited the church. It was a big surprise to come out of the church to an entire parade band. The band escorted them all the way to the reception, playing marching music. That was only the beginning. At the reception, a tractor trailer pulled up and unloaded a camel and an elephant.

"It's true," said Mickey. "I am probably the only person on earth who had camel and elephant rides at my wedding reception!" When Cindy, Jerry's other sister, got married, Jerry and his brothers showed up at the reception in full animal costumes. Jerry was the gorilla!

Even when they were young, there were a lot of practical jokes among the cousins and brothers and sisters. Jerry put seaweed on his sister's head and she got back at him by putting a jellyfish down his bathing suit. The brothers would dare each other to eat the little green crabs, live, and they would do it! Yes, Jerry did it too.

Jerry has clever ways of letting his family know that he is thinking about them. During assemblies he has referred to the goosefish page in *The Ocean Alphabet Book* as, "my favorite page in the book because it looks like my sister."

One day a boy said, "I'm going to tell your sister you said that!" Jerry thought that was a great idea. Now he gives his sister's address to hundreds of school children with the assignment to please write her and tell her that her bald-headed brother misses her and thinks she looks like a goosefish.

May 22, 1992

Dear Mickey,
    Jerry said you look like a goosefish! He showed us the picture. I think you probably don't look like that.

Sincerly Yours,
Amanda

P.S. I love your brothers looks
P.P.S He came into day because of young authors.

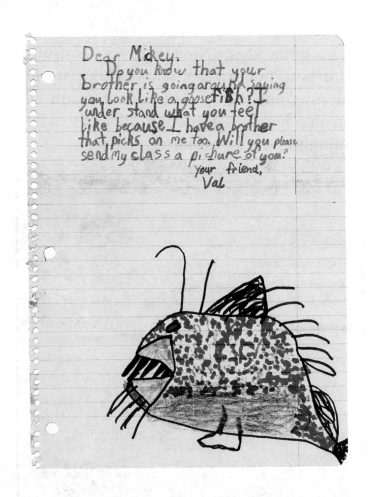

Dear Mickey,
Do you know that your brother is going around saying you look like a goosefish? I understand what you feel like because I have a brother that picks on me too. Will you please send my class a picture of you?
your friend,
Val

Sometimes someone in Jerry's family starts the joke. Jerry's Uncle Tony noticed that Jerry's children were in some of the illustrations in his books. Uncle Tony later noticed that many of the cousins were showing up in Jerry's books. Since his children were grown, he decided that he wanted his dog, Beckie, to have her picture in a book too. Jerry did not have a page for an Irish Setter in any of the books so he had to tell his uncle, "No." Uncle Tony didn't give up. He decided that maybe Jerry's mother could convince him to put Beckie in a book. She couldn't. Then Uncle Tony talked to Jerry's grandmother and tried to get her to convince Jerry, too. Nothing worked.

Uncle Tony started a petition that said, "I think Beckie the Dog should be in one of Jerry Pallotta's books." He walked up and down the beach one day getting people to sign their names.

Uncle Tony waited until a big moment to present the petition. The Boston Globe newspaper was interviewing Jerry at a bookstore when he barged in and said, "Here's the petition. Please put Beckie in one of your books!" The petition was five feet long and had five hundred signatures!

Jerry was working on *The Icky Bug Counting Book* at the time. It is a counting book but it is also a backwards alphabet book. The pages read zero through twenty-six. Then, if you go through the book backwards, the names of the bugs are in alphabetical order. Jerry couldn't figure out how to get Beckie into a bug book, until he wrote the page for the number twenty-one, which also happens to be the F page. Then he knew exactly what to do. Jerry wrote, "How did this dog sneak into this book? This Irish Setter has twenty-one fleas. You cannot count them because fleas are so tiny that they are really hard to find. This dog should take a bath and get a flea collar."

Now when Jerry visits schools he tells the children that the dog in the book is his uncle's dog and that her name is Beckie Pallotta. He also tells them that they can write Beckie Pallotta and he gives out his uncle's address. Children from around the United States have been writing Uncle Tony with suggestions for Beckie's flea problem.

4/9/92

Dear Becky,
    I am so sorry that you have so many fleas.
I bet you don't like them, I wouldn't either. I'm sure
that you look pretty with fleas anyways So don't feel bad.
Do you like being in that counting book? I bet you are
a very good dog. I'm just wondering do you swim?

                    Sincerly,
                        Laura

P.S. My cat's said, "Hi"!

101

It has never been unusual for Jerry to do the unexpected. After his brother, David, had not caught a lobster in several weeks, Jerry bought a huge plastic lobster and sneaked it into one of his traps. He has arrived at Thanksgiving dinner with a live turkey on a leash. Once, he came for Christmas dinner with fifty sets of foam antlers and red noses for a family "Rudolph" picture. He has greeted a friend at the airport with a professional juggling act. During assemblies full of children, he has given parts of his talks with a live lobster crawling on his head.

A reporter once wrote, "Jerry seems like a child trapped in a man's body."

Wherever Jerry Pallotta goes, he does seem to spread a fun-loving mania. After an assembly at a school one day, a young child told him, "You're not a writer, you're a comedian!" Part of that is true. He loves to make people laugh and he especially loves to hear the laughter of children. But he is also a writer.

"I never thought I would be a writer,"

said Jerry. "I was interested and fascinated at first to see if I could write a book. Then I realized that I found an idea that fit my personality. I found that I love to do research. I love to work with illustrators and I love to promote my books."

As a result, he will probably continue to think up ideas for new books. He will probably continue to visit schools across the United States and make children laugh. And he will probably always be chasing the letters of the alphabet.

Chapter
14

J is for Jerry

A a

A is for Author Cards of America. Jerry designed author and illustrator cards that are like baseball trading cards. On the front is a picture and on the back is information about the author or illustrator. Jerry hands his author card out to children when he visits schools. One day he saw a group of girls together, laughing and giggling. When he asked them what was so funny, they showed him one of his author cards. The girls had drawn a full head of hair on his picture. Jerry hopes that someday children will collect author and illustrator cards like they collect sports cards. He says, "Sports are great but reading is better."

B b

B is for Best Bird Book. In 1987 the *Bird Alphabet Book* was voted "One of the Best Books of the Year" by Birder's World Magazine. B is also for Bald. You only have to look at Jerry Pallotta's author card to know why bald is included in this alphabet. Some people think it is good luck to rub a bald person's head.

C c

C is for Cockroach. When Jerry was researching the *Icky Bug Alphabet Book*, Donald Salvatore, an insect specialist at the Museum of Science in Boston, let Jerry hold and pet a Hissing Cockroach from Madagascar. It was as long as his hand!

D d

D is for Dentist. Jerry says he finds ideas for alphabet letters in the most unlikely places. Once, after getting a dental checkup, his dentist, Dr. Duffell, gave him a toothbrush shaped like a crocodile. The toothbrush box told about a bird that cleans the teeth of a crocodile while the crocodile holds its mouth open! Jerry checked with Brian Cassie at the Audubon Society, who confirmed the information. In *The Bird Alphabet Book*, C is for Crocodile Bird. Jerry thanked Dr. Duffell by giving him a framed print of the Crocodile Bird page to hang in his office.

E e

E is for Eagle-Hoya. Jerry went to Boston College High School. Students there call themselves "eagles." Jerry loved his high school and his son Neil is named after his favorite high school teacher, Father Neil Callahan, S.J. Jerry went to business school at Georgetown University. Students there call themselves "hoyas," so Jerry is an Eagle-

Hoya. He says, "I owe these two schools a million thanks for a wonderful education."

E is also for Ethel. Ethel was a lobster that Jerry and his cousins adopted for a pet. Sometimes they would take her for walks up and down Peggotty Beach on a leash.

F f

F is for Favorite Books. Jerry's favorite alphabet book is *On Market Street* by Anita Lobel. Some of his other favorite books are *The Very Hungry Caterpillar* by Eric Carle, *Alaska's Three Bears* by Shelley Gill, and *Quick as a Cricket* by Audrey and Don Wood. Jerry's favorite adult books are true survival stories like *Adrift* (76 Days Lost at Sea) by Stephen Callahan or *The Breach* (Kilimanjaro and the Conquest of Self) by Rob Taylor. Jerry also likes to read nonfiction books like *Digging Dinosaurs* by Jack Horner.

G g

G is for Gerbils. Jerry's brother Joe wanted to play a practical joke on Jerry at Jerry's wedding. He bought two gerbils from a pet shop and was going to hide them under the cups at the places where Jerry and Linda would sit at their wedding dinner. The plan backfired. The gerbils escaped in Joe's car before the dinner. Over the next few months, Joe found many holes in his car seats but he never found the gerbils.

H h

H is for Heroes. Jerry always admired the astronauts when he was young. They were his heroes. He still remembers meeting Frank Borman, one of the Apollo astronauts, who came to his school. Jerry thought the astronauts were brave, smart and tough.

I i

I is for Ideas. Jerry thinks the most exciting thing about writing is coming up with an idea, researching it, and discovering that no one has ever written a book about it before.

I is also for The Icky Bugs. When Jerry coached his daughter's indoor soccer team, the girls voted to call themselves The Icky Bugs. The team logo was the Elephant Stag Beetle and was imprinted on their shirts.

J j
J is for Joe Doherty. Joe Doherty is a childhood friend of Jerry's. They have known each other since kindergarten. Although Joe is a lawyer, not an editor, he often previews and edits some of Jerry's books before they are published. *The Furry Alphabet Book* is dedicated to Joe Doherty. Jerry says he is a funny guy and a great storyteller.

K k
K is for Killer Whale. Killer Whales are Jerry's favorite animal. He thinks they are beautiful and intelligent. Jerry never real-

ized how big a whale was until he stood on Peggotty Beach next to a humpback whale that had died and washed ashore. Jerry said, "It was bigger than a school bus."

L l

L is for Leslie Evans. Leslie is the talented illustrator who illustrated *The Flower Alphabet Book*. Leslie has her own printing press in her basement that she uses for special projects. She sets the type by hand, letter by letter. She sometimes prints from linoleum blocks that she has cut with designs or pictures. She makes books on her press for herself and her family. Once, she created an alphabet book that featured her dog, Morgan, posed in the shape of each letter. Leslie is currently illustrating another book by Jerry. It is an alphabet book about herbs, spices and other natural flavors. Can you guess what the title will be?

M m

M is for Martha and Arthur. Martha and Arthur are two rocks that can only be seen at low tide in Peggotty Bay. Jerry used to moss off these rocks. Someday he wants to write a story about Martha and Arthur.

N n

N is for Northeaster. A northeaster is a storm that blows from the northeast. Jerry remembers the northeaster blizzard in 1978 when waves were breaking over the houses on Peggotty Beach. Homes were destroyed and the town of Scituate was flooded. After the storm, Jerry remembers walking through the town and seeing boats and living room furniture scattered in the streets. He also remembers walking on the beach and seeing a sandy lot where a house used to be. Jerry's dory vanished in the 1978 northeaster and he never found it.

O o

O is for Ocean Alphabet Trilogy. Jerry has already written the first two books of The Ocean Alphabet Trilogy. His first book, *The Ocean Alphabet Book* is about creatures from the Atlantic Ocean. *The Underwater Alphabet Book* is about tropical fish that live in warm water coral reefs. He will complete the three-book series when he finishes *The Pacific Ocean Alphabet Book*.

P p

P is for Peanut Butter Pizza. During his travels around the United States, Jerry has tried many unusual foods. He has eaten coffee jello, fiddlehead ferns, boiled peanuts, pickled cow's tongue, crawfish, squid ink spaghetti, fish tacos and garlic ice cream. Jerry has liked almost all of the foods he has tried but he says the worst thing he has ever tasted was peanut butter and banana pizza. It was made with pizza crust, peanut butter, bananas, tomato sauce, and cheese. Icky and yucky!

Q q

Q is for Questions. Children have asked Jerry some interesting questions.

One boy who had never heard a Boston accent, asked, "Are you an American?"

Jerry answered, "Of course. But my parents are aliens from the planet Alphabetron."

Another child asked, "When are you going to write a real book, instead of an alphabet book?"

Jerry answered, "When I grow up."

Many children have asked, "How do you write the words so neat in the books?"

Jerry explains that the printing in the books is not his handwriting. The books are printed by a machine. Jerry's handwriting is actually very messy!

R r

R is for Ruth Heller. Ruth Heller is a children's author who inspired Jerry. She was one of the first authors to write and illustrate picture books on nonfiction topics, specifically on nature. Jerry remembers reading

Chickens Aren't The Only Ones by Ruth Heller to his young children before he ever wrote his first book.

S s

S is for Swordfish Noses. Jerry travels with the sword-shaped noses of a swordfish and a sawfish. They are over three feet long. During assemblies, he holds the noses up to children's faces to see what they would look like with a swordfish or a sawfish nose. At airports, he frequently has trouble when the noses go through the x-ray machines. The security people ask him a lot of questions. Jerry politely explains that he is an author who uses the swords for educating children about sea creatures. One security guard did not believe that the swords were from fish until Jerry let him smell them.

T t

T is for Think Big. Jerry's brother, Joe, always encouraged Jerry to Think Big. When Jerry was writing his first books, Joe gave him the confidence to pursue his other book ideas. "Imagine if I had listened to people who told me to wait a couple of years to see how the first book did before I wrote another," said Jerry.

U u

U is for Uncle Sonny. Uncle Sonny is Arthur Pallotta. He is Jerry's uncle and a scientist. He thinks school children should know more about science at a young age. He is always coming up with ideas for Jerry. For instance, Uncle Sonny wants Jerry to write a book on atoms.

V v

V is for *The Victory Garden Alphabet Book*. Jerry wrote *The Victory Garden Alphabet Book* with Bob Thomson. When Jerry was a boy, his father listened to Bob Thomson's Garden Show on the radio. "I remember trying to change the station so I could hear The Beatles," said Jerry. "But my Dad would make me switch the station back to Bob's show." For many years, Bob Thomson was also the host of The Victory Garden television show on PBS. After meeting Bob, Jerry decided he was one of the nicest people he had ever met. He was thrilled when Bob agreed to co-author *The Victory Garden Alphabet Book*.

W w
W is for Wonderful Parents. Jerry and his brothers and sisters all seem to agree that they have wonderful parents.

X x
X is for *Xiphias gladius*. *Xiphias gladius* is the scientific name for swordfish. About a year after *The Ocean Alphabet Book* was published, a friend of Jerry's told him that his eight-year-

old son loved the book. The boy, Evan Meagher, knew all the ocean creatures in the book from reading it over and over again. Evan went to a restaurant with his parents one evening and after studying the menu, confidently said to the waitress "I'll have *Xiphias gladius* for dinner, please."

Yy

Y is for Young Authors' Fairs. Jerry has visited many Young Authors' Fairs. He has looked at hundreds of books that are written by children. Jerry says, "I don't ever remember writing a book or a journal when I was in elementary school. I think it's really great that children are encouraged to write."
Jerry has visited over 300 schools in the United States. His goal is to speak in schools in all fifty states.

Z z

Z is for Zillion. The word "zillion" is in the text on every Z page in all of Jerry Pallotta's alphabet books. A zillion is an extremely large number. It is so large that you cannot count how many a zillion actually is. It would be hard to guess how many words Jerry has researched, how many school children he has met, or how many smiles he has spread. Probably a zillion.

Books by Jerry Pallotta

About the Author of
"About the Author Books"

Pamela Ryan, MA. Ed., was born and grew up in the San Joaquin Valley in Bakersfield, California. A graduate of San Diego State University, she has been living in Leucadia, California since 1975. She is the author of books for adults and children and often visits schools and teacher's conferences to speak about writing and literacy. One of her presentations, "Everybody Has a Story," encourages children to journal and to write their own autobiographies and stories from their life experiences.

Her household, near the Pacific Ocean, includes her husband, children (Marcy, Annie, Tyler and Matt), two Corn snakes, and two dogs. *Chasing the Alphabet* is her fourth book.